Sto

Prepared under the direction of
Illa Podendorf
Laboratory School, University of Chicago

Ninety-eight per cent of the text is in words from
the Combined Word List for Primary Reading

the true book of

FARM ANIMALS

by JOHN LEWELLEN
illustrated by
DWIGHT MUTCHLER

CHILDRENS PRESS, CHICAGO

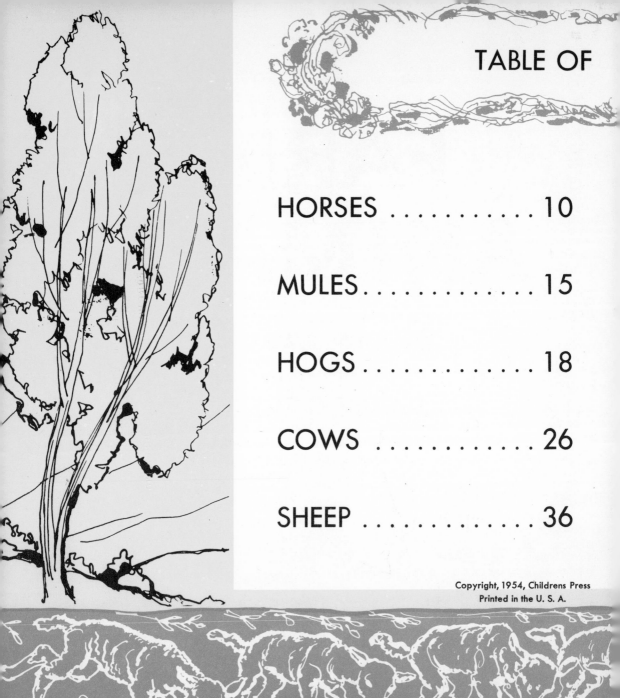

TABLE OF

CONTENTS

PLAN OF DADDY TOM'S FARM

OATS

WHEAT

CORN

WOODS

PASTURE

SOY BEANS

PASTURE

HOG HOUSES & LOT

BARN

BARN

FEED

TOOLS

HOME

PASTURE

POULTRY YARD

GARDEN

ORCHARD

ROAD

My father lives on a farm.
His name is Daddy Tom.
This is Daddy Tom's farm.

Daddy Tom loved horses.
The ones he liked best
    were May and Belle.
They worked together.
They were a team.
May and Belle were little.
But they liked to pull big
    loads.
Daddy Tom would talk to
    his horses.
He never used a whip.

One day four big horses
could not pull a truck
out of the mud.
May and Belle did it.
They knew how to pull
together.

May and Belle liked to roll
in the pasture grass.
Sometimes they would run
and play.

Daddy Tom still loves horses. But he does not need them now. He does all his work with a tractor.

This is much faster.

In the South, mules are
used more than horses.
Mules will not work too
hard on a hot day.
Horses sometimes do.
Then they get sick.

The mother of a baby mule
is a horse, a mare.
The father is a donkey.
The baby mule looks
like both.

MARE

BABY
MULE

DONKEY

Daddy Tom takes good care
   of all his animals.
He is kind to them.
He says that any farmer
   who is kind can make
   pets of all farm animals.
Daddy Tom likes his hogs
   best of all.

When he goes to their field
they follow him.

Hogs can not sweat the way we do. On hot days they must find other ways to cool off, or they will die. They like to lie in clean water to keep cool.
If there is no clean water, they must lie in mud holes.

Hogs like to keep clean.
And they never eat too much.
Daddy Tom keeps food in
front of his pigs all
the time.

SALT

CORN

They eat just as much as they need. They always eat the right kinds of food.
Something seems to tell them what is best for them.

MINERALS

MIXED GRAIN

One of Daddy Tom's mother
hogs has nine baby pigs.

Some baby pigs need
special care.

She has nine more pigs,
six months old. Each of
them weighs about 200
pounds.

There are many kinds of hogs.

CHESTER WHITE

HAMPSHIRE

DUROC-JERSEY

POLAND
CHINA

Mother cows have only one
   or two babies each year.
They are called "calves."
The babies weigh about
   100 pounds.
The calves grow up. They
   have babies of their
      own when they are two

                     years old.

1 HOUR OLD

3 DAYS OLD

This calf's mother is
two years old.
Its grandmother is four
years old. Its great
grandmother is six
years old.

Cows have no front upper
teeth. This makes it
easy for them to eat
grass.
Some have horns.
Some do not.

Cows can eat grass
without chewing it,
because they have four
stomachs.
They pick lots of grass
while the day is cool.

During the hot part of the
day, cows lie in the
shade. Then they chew
the grass they have
eaten.
The little balls of grass
come back to their mouths.

This is the way cows are
milked by hand.
Cows are milked each
morning and evening.

Farmers with many cows
use milking machines.
This is easier and faster.
The farmer washes the cow
with warm water before
using the milking
machine.

Most of Daddy Tom's cows
let him use the milking
machine.
But Maude did not.
So Daddy Tom let three
little lambs milk Maude.
Maude took the mother sheep's
place.
The newspapers ran pictures
of the new family.

GUERNSEY

BROWN
SWISS

JERSEY

HOLSTEIN

There are many kinds of cows.

BUTTER

ICE CREAM

Many things are
made from milk
and cream.

CHEESE

BABY FOODS

GLUE

PAINT

PLASTICS

BALLOONS

Daddy Tom has lots of sheep.
They have coats of wool
  to keep them warm.
They eat grass and even
  weeds.
Sheep are like cows. They
  have no upper front teeth.
They have four stomachs, too.
Baby lambs are very cute.
They like to jump and play.

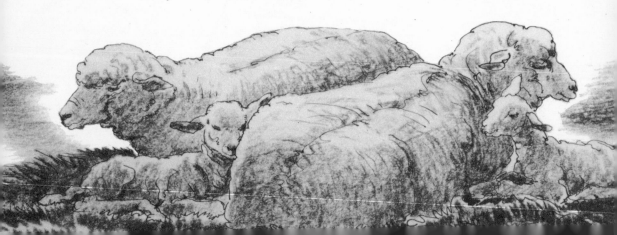

One day Daddy Tom was too
tired to cut his grass
He let his sheep do it
for him.

Sheep give us wool.
The wool is used to make
warm clothes and blankets.
There is oil in the wool.
The oil is used in many
things.

Daddy Tom cuts the wool
from the sheep when the
weather is warm.

By the time cold weather
comes, the sheep will
have grown new coats.

Some farmers keep goats.
Goats sometimes play all
    day.
They climb and jump and
    bump their heads
    together.
Goats' milk is used
    for cheese.

People sometimes drink goats' milk, too.
Daddy Tom has lots of chickens.
Chickens have no teeth. They eat little stones to help grind up their food.
Most of the year, Daddy Tom's hens lay one egg a day.

Sometimes Daddy Tom has ducks and geese and turkeys.

He has a cat to catch the
mice and rats.
He has a dog that helps
bring in the cows at
milking time.
Horses, cows, sheep and
hogs, ducks and chickens,
cats and dogs—
Daddy Tom takes good care
of all his animals.